An Dhargan a
The Prophecy of Merlin

Jowann Kernow
John of Cornwall

Dyllans kernewek ha sowsnek gans

Edition in Cornish and English by

Julyan Holmes

Kesva an Taves Kernewek,
The Cornish Language Board 1998

Daswelys hag ewnhes Mis Hedra
2nd edition, revised, October 2001

Kudhlenn (cover picture): Tamsyn Moore

ISBN 1 902917 197

Contents

English on left-hand pages	***Kernewek a-dheghow***
Foreword	**Raglavar**
John of Cornwall	**Jowann Kernow**
The Manuscript	**An Vammskrif**
Merlin	**Merdhin**
p2. The Prophecy of Merlin	**f.1 An Dhargan a Verdhin**
Background reading	**Livrow dhe les**

Raglavar

Par dell o dynyes an ankredoryon vor dre *Dir an Gwinbrennyer*, (Amerika), yn kettella, maga skon dell wodhvev yn hy hever, an Dhargan Gernewek a Verdhin a'm tenna kepar ha pan ve tennven! Kavoes golok anedhi, ha, dres ken, dos dh'y honvedhes, (mar bell dell ylliv), honna a veu dhymm vyaj hir, kepar dell o, dhedha i, an Mor Bras.

Gwynn ow bys, ytho, kavoes gweres a'n wonisogeth lyverji yn Kernow, a'n Lyverji Predennek, ha dhiworth Dr. Oliver Padel y'n Fondyans a Studhyansow Kernewek. Dre weres a'n par na, chons a'm beu dhe hwithra nebes lyvrow tanow ha drudh rag igeri an destenn. Dhy'hwi oll, 'Meur ras dhy'hwi!', hag ynwedh dhe Keith Syed, Jori Ansell ha Graham Sandercock. Dhe Leonard Boyle, O.P., y'n Vatikan, neb a brovias skeusenn a'n mammskrif, 'Go raibh maith agat!'

Orth penn an lyver, y kevir henwyn nebes lyvrow dhe les.

Herwydh Jowann, y treylyas ev hen vammskrif, a'n taves Brythonek dhe Latin, may halla moy pobel y redya!
Gwrys veu henna orth gorholedh Robert Warelwast, Epskop Keresk.
Skrifa yn Latin o martesen gwryans fur y'n eur na;
dhyn ni, hedhyw yn jydh, nyns yw meur dhe les;
dyllans arnowydh genen o mall.

An hen vammskrif a biwo Jowann re dalvia bos
kynsa skrifys a-dro dhe'n vlydhen 950.
Dhiworth kampoellansow istorek yn y notennow, y synsir Jowann dhe skrifa y dreylyans ynter 1140 ha 1155, pan verwis an epskop.

Rag henna, homm yw an kottha rann a lyenn kernewek eus genen ni. Kernewek a'y thestenn hag a'y skrifer, mes ynwedh a'y yeth — Jowann a re dhyn lies dyth berr yn '*Brythonek*', (kernewek) dhiworth an kyns-skrif. Leon Fleuriot, an skoler bretonek a vri, a verkyas an talvos arbennik a biw an skrif dre henna; tanow yw ynter an kuntelles a skrifow gelwys 'An Vater a Vreten', rag y vos gwithys, yn rann, y'n taves teythyek.
Dhyn ni yn Kernow, y provi golok dhibarow yn preder den dyskys, genesik a Gernow, gwlas esa hwath ow pystiga a drygh a-gynsow an Sowson hag, yn dydhyow Jowann, ow kodhevel paynys an vresel ynter Stephen ha Matilda.

Acknowledgements

Just like 'Vinland', (America), attracted the Vikings, so, as soon as I knew about it, the Cornish Prophecy of Merlin drew me, like a magnet!

Getting to read the original text and understand it, as far as I have been able to, was a long voyage, like the Atlantic, for them.

Fortunately, Cornwall's wonderful Library Service, the British Library and Dr. Oliver Padel at the Institute of Cornish Studies, gave me access to the rare and expensive background material I needed

To them all, a Cornish 'Thanks' - Meur ras dhy'hwi! and to Leonard E. Boyle, O.P., in the Vatican Library, for a photocopy of the original manuscript, 'Go raibh maith agat!' Grateful thanks also, to Keith Syed, Graham Sandercock and Jori Ansell for their assistance in preparing this work for publication.

Foreword

According to John, he translated an ancient manuscript from the British language, (i.e. the ancestor of Cornish, Welsh and Breton), into Latin, '*so that more people would be able to read it*'! This at the request of Robert Warelwast, then Bishop of Exeter, to whom he wrote a humble dedication. Writing in Latin may have made sense in 1140; to most of us, nowadays, it is not a great help and it was definitely time for a modern edition.

John's manuscript source must originally have dated from about 950 AD. From historical references in his notes, it is thought John's version was produced between 1140 and 1155, when Warelwast died.

This makes it the oldest surviving piece of Cornish literature, — Cornish, not just because of its subject-matter, nor even because it was written here, but because John, in his notes, gives us several extracts in the original language.

The Breton scholar, Leon Fleuriot, pointed out the special value of that feature; it is unusual, amongst a large body of documents, known as 'The Matter of Britain', in preserving fragments of the original vernacular.

For us, in Cornwall, it provides a unique insight on the thoughts of an educated Cornishman, in a nation still smarting from recent conquest by the English, and currently enduring the hardships of the civil war, (1135-7), between Stephen and the Empress Matilda.

Jowann Kernow

Jowann Kernow, (Iohannis Cornubiensis, alias Iohannis de Sancto Germano) a veu genys, yn hevelep, yn Lannales, (Plu Jerman), a-var y'n dewdhegves kansblydhen. Wosa studhya yn Paris, gans Thierri de Chartres, hag yn Rom, y tegemmeras M.A.. Y hanow a veu kampoellys avel den gwiw dhe vos Epskop Tyddewi yn Kembra, drefenn ev dhe wodhvos an yeth kembrek. Dell hevel, skonys veu rag an keth skila; ny vynna an Myghtern gorra y'n se epskop a alla krevhe an kaskyrgh a-barth Arghepskobeth. kembrek. Marow veu a -dro dhe'n vlydhen 1199.

Skoler a vri o va; y kavas Michael Curley, y'n notennow, dyth a'n prydydh klassek, Horas (Horace). Hanow da a'n jevo rag gormeula an Pab Alexander III, may skrifas erbynn Peder Abelard. Nyns eus skila vydh rag perthi dout na alla Jowann treylya skrifa Brythonek yn 'heksametrow' Latin flowr.

Heb dhout, yth aswonni nebes a'n profoesa hen gembrek - an keth daffar a wrug Jeffri devnydh anodho. Rag henna, yma taklow kemmyn dhe'n dhiw dhargan. Nebes skolheygyon a wogrysis na wrella Jowann namoy es das-skrifa rann a oberenn Jeffri — An Istori a'n Vyghternedh a Vreten. Byttegyns yma moy es unn skila rag krysi dhe Jowann.
Yn kynsa, hwath pan yw kehaval an dhew brofoesa, ny syw pub tymmik y'n keth tyller; Dhe voy a vri: yn unn tyller, dhe'n liha, diffransow yntra'n dhew a syw lavarow diblans y'ga mammskrif. Rag ensampel, Jeffri a skrifas liesplek 'karn', le may hworras Jowann 'korn'. An dhew er a allas bos pur es kammskrifys an eyl rag y gila.
Dres ken, yth yw an dythow ma, yn Brythonek hen, (po *kernewek*), neb a brev bos dhe Jowann y hen vammskrif y honan.

Mar nyns yw marth klywes ha krev o kas, gans Jowann, an Sowson, dhe les yw gweles fatell omglywo, den a Gernow, gans an gembryon ha'n vretonyon, rann an wlas vrythonek, an *Britannia*, esa ena kyns dos an sowson dhiworth Almayn. Sowdhenys via lies redyor ow kweles an Normanyon, synsys dhe vos *keffrysysi* yn dial an bobel deythyek war an fethoryon.

John of Cornwall

Iohannis Cornubiensis, (John of Cornwall), *alias* Iohannis de Sancto Germano), was probably born at Lannales, (i.e. St. Germans), in South East Cornwall, early in the twelfth century.

Studying in Paris, with Thierry de Chartres, and in Rome, he obtained an M.A.. His name was later put forward as a candidate to be Bishop of Tyddewi, (St. David's), in Wales, on account of his knowledge of the language. It seems he was rejected for that very reason: the King did not want him to add weight to the campaign for a Welsh Archbishopric.

He died in around 1199.

He was a renowned scholar; Michael Curley found, in John's notes, a quotation from the classical Latin poet, Horace. He was celebrated for a eulogy of Pope Alexander III, in which he argued against the views of the great Peter Abelard. There is, then, no reason to doubt John's ability to translate a document in the old British language into good Latin hexameters.

John had certainly read the Old Welsh prophecies, including some of the material that Geoffrey of Monmouth worked from. There are, naturally, many points in common, where prophecies in John's poem are to be found in the early part of the 'Prophecies' section of Geoffrey's *'History of the Kings of Britain'*.

For this reason, some scholars suspected John of merely paraphrasing Geoffrey.

But, while he almost certainly read Geoffrey, (the 'best-seller' of his day), there are good reasons for believing John's claim. For one thing, even when more or less identical, the prophecies are not necessarily in the same order. Secondly, in at least one place, differences appear to arise from divergences in the copies used as sources. Such as where John translated a word as '*hooves*', while Geoffrey wrote '*horns*'. It has been suggested that this may be due to the similarity of the two Celtic words, *karn* - hoof, and *korn* - horn, either of which might have been miss-copied for the other.

> These extracts, in Old British and Cornish, are, in themselves, convincing support for the existence of John's own ancient source.

If it is no surprise to see the hatred John felt towards the Saxons, it is interesting to see how a Cornishman regarded himself, along with the Welsh and the Bretons, a part of the British Nation, that is of the *Britannia* that existed before the Saxons invaded from Germany.

It may come as a shock, though, to find the Normans considered as *allies*, playing a vital role in the native population's revenge on the English colonists.

Such political prophecies could be double-edged weapons: In Wales and Ireland, Norman war-leaders took copies with them. taking pains to 'fulfil' them as much as possible, so that their foes could see defeat predicted for them in their own texts.

Merdhin

Pan skrifas Jeffri Monow y 'istori', rag redyoryon Normanek,
y ti'velebis an hanow Kembrek, Myrddhin, yn *Merlin*,
may fe dhe esya yn ganowow Frynkegoryon.
Gwell yw genev furv nes dhe'n Kembrek, (*dh* = an *dd* yn Kembrek).

Yn lyenn Keltek, y teuth ha bos dew 'Verdhin':
Myrddin Emrys, (po *Ambrosius*), an huni usi Jowann ow kampoella omma,
ha Myrddin Sylvester, (po '*Celyddon*', (Caledonia).

Ny vern henna dhyn ni; yth o, dell grysav, an keth den,
ha'y hwedhel, dre vras, par dell syw:
Pennsevik Keltek o Merdhin, dell dybir, yn neb tiredh yn Alban deghow.
Gyllys 'mes a'y skians dre ladhva a'n Gas a *Arfdderydh*, yth eth dhe vos
koelyek.

Trigys y'n koes, y teuth ha bos Arloedh war an miles gwyls; dres ken,
war an kerwys.
Lies profoesa a veu, dell dherivir, gwrys ganso;
yntredha, gwersyow kembrek: 'an avalennow'
ha'n '*oianau*' — (kuntelles ankenegow).
Kernow, Breten Vyghan ha Kembra a wra kwarel ragdho, poran kepar dell
wrons rag Arthur meur.

Nessa folenn a'n mammskrif, styryansow Yowann Kernow a-dheghow hag yn-dann an tekst	*The second page of the manuscript, with John of Cornwall's explanations to the right of the text and below.*

Foto Biblioteca Apostolica Vaticana

An Mammskrif

Nyns usi an mammskrif ma dhe weles yn Kernow na tyller vydh yn Breten Veur; y'n gwithir aji dhe Lyverji an Vatikan. Martesen, wosa bos selyes an Bennskol a Gernow, y hyllir gwaytya y fydh daskerrys **Ottobianus Latinus** 1474, (fols. 1r - 4r) dhe'gan gwlas ni.

Awos oll y vos skrifys neb mil vlydhen alemma, ny veu gwelys an skrif ma, nans o eth kansblydhen, y'gan yeth ni.

Na, dhe'm gwella godhvos, ny omdhiskwedhas namoy es nebes dythow berr yn sowsnek . An Latin a veu dyllys yn 1838, gans Karl Greith yn Almayn, ha treylyans frynkek arnowydh gans Leon Fleuriot, neb ugens blydhen alemma.

An gwella dyllans a'n Latin a veu gans Michael Curley yn Amerika. Honn yw an destenn a wrug evy dhe sywya.

[Dyllo profoesa gwlasek yw gwryans dyantell; hag yn Kembra hag yn Iwerdhon, an hembrenkysi lu Normanek a dheuth gans dasskrifow an profoesa teythyek; gwella gallens, y hwilsens aga 'hollenwel' may hwella an eskerens aga fetha, darleverys gans aga thus fur aga honan].

Ottomma, a'y wosa, rann nebes aswonnys a istori Gwlas Kernow:

Troes-notennow:

MS	Mammskrif
f.	folenn an mammskrif
l.	linenn an mammskrif
JK	notenn gans Jowann Kernow
JGH	notenn gans Julyan Holmes

Merlin

When Geoffrey of Monmouth wrote his 'history', for a Norman readership, he altered Welsh 'Myrddin' to 'Merlin', less of a 'mouthful' for French-speakers. I prefer a form closer to the Welsh; (*dh*, like Welsh *dd*, sounds like *th* in '*th*is').

There came to be, in literature, two *Merlins*: Myrddin Emrys, (or Ambrosius), the one mentioned by John, and Myrddin Sylvester, of Caledonia.

They were, however, probably one and the same. The outline of his story runs as follows: Merlin, a Celtic chieftain, probably in what is now Southern Scotland, was driven mad by the slaughter at the battle of *Arfdderydd*. He became a hermit, seer, or *shaman*. Living in the forests, he became Lord of the Animals, especially of the stags. Many prophecies, throughout the Celtic world, were attributed to him, such as the Welsh verses called the '*Afallenau*', (apple-trees), and the '*oianau*', a series of laments.

Cornwall, Brittany and Wales each have a claim on Merdhin, as on Arthur.

Though first written more than a thousand years ago, my recent version, in Cornish, was probably the first time it had been seen in our language for eight centuries. Nor had more than a few short passages been published in English, prior to my bilingual edition, though one in French appeared in the 1970s. The Latin text was first published by Karl Greith in Germany, in 1838 but I have based these translations on the American, Michael Curley's, 1985, revised version.

Here, then, is unique testimony to the little-known National History of Kernow.

Julyan Holmes, July 1998. 2nd Edition 2001.

Key to footnotes to the text:

MS	refers to the manuscript itself
P,	page of the manuscript
l.	line of the manuscript
JC	note by John of Cornwall
JGH	note by Julyan Holmes.

An Dhargan a Verdhin

A Howldrevel[1], an Hanterdydh a gach dhe ves
dha eginyow dhiworth agan lowarthow
hag a syns neb a dallo toll
avel ensampel rag an toller.
Tremena a wra yn prenn[2], diwysek ha gwyskys yn horn;
yth omladh y'n gwel, omwithys yn kaspows triflek,
kenedhel, worboellek yn breselyow,
mall gensi ladhva an Sowson.

An re na, a rolla aga ober
a-gynsow dhe rakyow hag ereder,
na sparyens aga Mamm mes hedhens yn hy glas!
Mar pe myns a'ga drogober an yew a gethneth, y's talons dhe vrasva[3],
na ny res dhymm kemmeres meth rag perthi kov.
Ow tastrehevel agan re[4], pes blydhen y fydh byw an Pennsevik?
"Diwweyth seyth war seyth[5] a reknydh an keth niver".

Neustria[6] wyls, mamm dhe agh bals, gwynn dha vys
bos ow tevi Diw Dhragon[7], yn eryon an Dialer!
Wostalleth, war tu ha mernans an eyl, gwarak a ystynnir[8];
hy ben[9] a hwerth yn skeus morethek y hanow.
"Pedergweyth diw ha pymp blydhen[10], own a berthir ragdho".

---

1 howldrevel = an sowson, an hanterdydh = an Normanyon, JK
2 prenn = 'mergh brenn', i.e. gorholyon, JK
3 'an falsuri o 'Nos an kellili hir' pan wrug Hengist ha Horsa, ladha gwelhevin an Vrythonyon, hag i warbarth orth kevywi- JGH. MS folenn 1, l. 8
  'Brasyans, kynsa erbynn an Vrythonyon, ha nessa erbynn an Normanyon' -JK
4 'agan re' = 'an nebes bretonyon' - JK, neb a dheuth gans Gwilym, hembrenkys gans Alan Fergant, hag a dhegemmeras statys brentyn y'ga hen vammdir.
5 (2x7) +7, =21 blydhen; Gwilym a reynyas 1066-1087
6 hen hanow Frynk kledh.
7 William II, Rufus ha Robert II, Dug Normandi
8 W Rufus a veu ledhys dre seth, hag ef ow helghya,
9 'hy ben' = Robert, JC
10 (4x2) +5, =13 blydhen; W Rufus, 1087-1100.

The Prophecy of Merlin

O East Wind[1], the South Wind shall snatch away
your young shoots from out of our gardens
and shall take the taxed as a model for the taxer.

There shall cross in timber[2], eager and dressed in iron;
there shall fight in the field, protected in a triple coat of mail,
A nation filled with battle-fury,
mad for the slaughter of the English!

Those who, just lately, put their energy into rakes and ploughshares,
Let them not spare their mother
but reach right to her innermost parts!
If the sum of their offence was the Yoke of Slavery,
they owe that to treachery[3], nor am I ashamed to recall it.

Raising up our own people[4], how many years will the Prince live?
'Twice seven, above seven[5], you will reckon the same number'.

Savage Normandy[6], mother of a fruitful progeny,
rejoice that there are, growing up, as heirs of the the Avenger,
Two Dragons[7].
Firstly, towards the death of the one, a bow is bending[8];
the Other One[9] laughs in the lugubrious shade of his name.
'Four times two, and five years[10], shall he be feared'.

---

1   The '*East Wind*' represents 'the Saxons', the '*South Wind*', the Normans, JC
2   '*timber*' means the '*wooden horses*', i.e. Norman ships', JC
3   The '*treachery*' was the 'Night of the Long Knives', when Hengist and Horsa's men, guests at a banquet, suddenly drew concealed weapons and killed three hundred of Vortigern's courtiers, JGH. JC says 'treacherous firstly towards the Britons, secondly towards the Normans'.
4   Flobert translated '*instaurans nostros*' by: 'reigning over our rulers', but JC refers in his notes to the 'few Bretons', under Alan Fergant, who landed with William the Conqueror and were well rewarded by him with estates in their former homeland, JGH.
5   (2x7) + 7 = 21 years, William reigned 1066- 1087.
6   John uses here an old name, *Neustria*, for the North of France.
7   The '*Two Dragons*' are William II (Rufus) and his brother, Robert II, Duke of Normandy.
8   William Rufus was killed by an arrow in a hunting accident.
9   The '*Other One*' is Robertus, JC.
10 (4x2) +5 = 13 years; William reigned 1087- 1100.

Hogen Lew Kompoester,
neb yw an gwella yn pub fordh, pur wir[11],
"Diwweyth seyth war eth, y hwra durya"[12],
yn unn wodreghi ewines an skoules
ha dens an bleydhes.
Y hwra saw an koesow ha saw an porthow a bub tu.
Hemma, peskweyth mayth usso,
y kren an touryow golghys dre dhowr Seina[13],
ha, bys y'n Mor Difeyth,
pub ynys an Dragones[14].

Ena an 'kryghys y vlew' a wra gwiska dillas brygh,
na ny wra dillas omwitha
rag hager oberow brys brottel.

Y'n eur na, owr a vydh gweskys
dhiworth an fionenn ha'n spernenn[15]
hag, a-dhia garnow[16] an re a beurro, y hwra dewraga.
Rakhenna, mynno kyn na vynno, trogh y bow[17],
an Harther a wra ambos orth an karow.

Furv mona a falser;
dhe hemma ynwedh, y hwra sywya an furv a gylgh lehes a hanter[18].

Wosa henna, war Araw, an Edhen a Veur Vri[19] a syns hy neyth
hag Alban a wra oela warlergh y lewigow[20]
a veu degys dhe ves.
Eghan! Pana dhrog ober an Mor
a dhre yn rag an trysa blydhen[21]
Seul na gemmerro truedh a vydh drog-eryes
rag y fellder triflek[22]!

---

11 Henricus, JK. (Henri I) . An Latin, a skrifas Jowann, a styrir yndellma, kynth hevel , a 'y notennow, ev y honan dhe gonvedhes an *grefni* a'n myghtern!
12 (2x7) +8, = 22 vlydhen *moy es reyn W Rufus* (13 blydhen). Henri I a reynyas 1100-1135.
    Jowann a re an niver na y'n kernewek a' y vammskrif : '*pemp bliden warn ugens ha hanter*'. y lever: 'Henn yw 25 + hanter ugens (=10)*: y hwra henna 35. nb: Da yw an kernewek, mes y'n taves a oes Jowann. Nyns yw hen gernewek - JGH.
13 Paris,
14 'kepar hag *Ybernia* (Iwerdhon), *Norwallia* (Kembra gledh), hag Alban' - JC
15 'dhiworth an da ha'n drog keffrys; lavarow a'n par ma yw kemmyn y'gan lyenn'- JK
16 Jeffri a re: '*kern*'; 'toll-benn' yw, pynag vo, war berghennieth gwarthek, JGH
17 Laghys fell a dhifennas gwitha helgeun yn ogas dhe bark gam ryal.
18 Towlennys veu batha mona nowydh: an '*demma*'.
19 An 'edhen' a dal bos an Emperes Matilda, 'neb a veu demmedhys dhe Heinrich V, yn Cologne, (yn gwirder, Mainz), ogas dhe'n avon *Aarau*, yn Almayn'.- JK
    Re erell a wel omma kas ogas dhe Eryri, (Snowdon), may feu fethys myghtern a Gembra, JGH
20 1120, pan veu beudhys an dhew bryns y'n 'Gorhel Gwynn'. JGH
21 'trysa blydhen reyn Gwilym o diwettha blydhen y vywnans', JK. Henna a dal bos an Pryns (na veu bythkweth yn gwiryonedh myghtern, JGH
22 'Triflek dre vos 'yn rann, Normanek, yn rann, Albanek, (?=Bretenek, JGH), hag, yn rann, sevys a woes agan gwelhevin ni', JK

But the Lion of Justice[11], who excels, truly, in all respects[12],
shall add 'twice seven, over eight'[13].
Trimming the claws of kites and the teeth of wolves.
he will make safe the forests and harbours on every hand.
Whenever this one roars, the towers that are washed by the River Seine[14]
shall tremble and, out in the ocean, each Island of Dragons[15].
Then, 'he of the crimped hair' shall put on multicoloured garments,
nor will his clothes protect him from the misdeeds of a fickle mind.

Then, gold will be expressed from the narcissus and the thorn[16]
and will pour from the hooves of grazing cattle.[17]

Therefore, willingly or not, with one paw cut off,
The Barker will make a treaty with the Stag[18].

The shape of money shall be divided;
to this, too, shall be added a circle reduced by half[19].

After that, on the Aarau, that Most Famous Bird shall sieze her nest[20]
and England will weep for her Cubs, who have been taken away[21].
Alas, what an awful Sea-crime the third year brings forth![22],
he that is without pity shall be infamous for his triple cruelty![23]

---

11 '*Henricus*', JC. (i.e. Henry I, not H II, as some commentators made out, JGH).
12 nb John's own Latin translates thus, but his notes, confusingly, imply that he thought it referred to Henry's greed.
13 (2x7) +8 = 22 years. i.e. he shall reign 22 yrs more than William Rufus' thirteen . Henry I reigned 1100-1135, i.e. thirty-five years. JC gives this figure, as from his source, in Cornish, but it is the Cornish of his own time, rather than of an ancient document, JGH.
14 i.e. *Paris*
15 'such as *Ybernia*, (Ireland), *Norwallia*, (North Wales), and Scotland, JC
16 i.e. 'from the bad and the good'. JC says 'this kind of metaphor is common in our poems'.
17 Geoffrey has 'from the *horns*'; in both cases, it means a 'poll tax' on cattle, JGH.
18 Refers to the harsh Norman hunting laws which reserved game parks for Royalty by forcing others nearby to cripple their hounds.
19 i.e. plans to mint a new coin - the halfpenny, JC .
20 The 'most famous Bird' is the Empress Matilda. JC explains that she married the Emperor, HeinrichV, at *Colonia*, (actually Mainz), near the Aarau, in Germany. An alternative theory is that *Aravium* in the original prophecy may be derived from Eryri, the Welsh name for Snowdon, where Henry I received the submission of a Welsh king in 1121. Henry's standard was ... an eagle.
21 This refers to 1120, when the two princes, William and Robert, sons of Henry I were drowned in the White Ship.
22 'The third year of his reign was the last of his life', JC. Presumably Prince William, The Atheling, who died in 1120, here included in the King-list? See Note 40, JGH; in 1116, Henry had made all the barons and prelates swear allegiance to William, as his successor, JC.
23 'Triple, because 'part Norman, part British , in *part arising from our own Cornish nobility*', JC

Yn dann an hwegh genesik a Bow Frynk, goes unnvamm[23],
trist, ow rudha, an Tron[24] neb a wodhevis
mar lies mernans, mar lies drog,
a gri ha gelwel yn mes:
'A Normani, a wodhesta pandr'a wrer?
A-gynsow, my a wodhevis, a-gynsow y tinewis ow glas[25]!
"Saw unnsel der an galarow ma,
ny redh hebaska dhe'gan galarow ni".
A Ynys[26], glyb warbarth osta gans dagrow!
Skant nyns eus myghtern vydh ha peub a vynn y vos.,
drefenn, re anvenowgh, y hwra devnydh a'n kledha!
Alemma rag, hemm yw an perghennek[27],
usi yn y gyrghynn euth rag an re fals;
askorr an Lew, kudhys y dal,
yn skeusow nos,
gorth arta, y kenki bys y'n ster.

An ambos terrys a elow
may sorro an Er gans an Lewik[28]
ha'n re na, a omgudh y'n koesow,
a dheu glan bys y'n fosow,
may hwrello an terewi[29] perthi own, unn jydh,
rag an re a vedha kas gansa i.
Kerensa vydh, po skant nyns eus, na hwath dyantell;
an dreyn a wordyv an helik[30].
Eghan! Re vras kummyas a rer dhe'n bleydhes ha dhe'n skoules.
"Teyrgweyth hwegh resegva ha tri, y hwra an oes ma durya.[31]"

---

23 Hwegh mab Toki, ledhys, yn 1106 wosa Krist, dre sordyans Kernowyon. An ledyer o *Vice-comes Frewin* ha'n tyller, Treruf, ?Treriefe, yn Madron -JK, Oliver Padel.
24 Kernow - JK; gelwys ynwedh *Chi Coronei*, warlergh koweth Brutus a Gerdroya, (Troy),. ha *Chi Arthur* (notenn 32)- JC
25 Rag mernans *Osulf* - JK Adro dhe 1106 w.k, (notenn 23) - JGH
26 'Breten Veur', JK
27 ? Stephen - JGH
28 Matilda ha'y mab - JK
29 = sitys, JK
30 'Sort trolavar kemmyn y'gan bardhonieth ni': *an dreyn* = 'an re dhrog' ha'n *helik*, an re nobyl, JK
31 Mars yw reyn Stephen, 3x6, +3 (=21), yw diw vlydhen re; martesen Stephen o hwath byw pan skrifas Jowann, JGH

Under the six natives of France, blood of one mother[24],
sorrowful and blushing, the Throne[25],
which has suffered so many deaths, so many evils,
shall cry out and exclaim:
Oh, Normandy[26], do you know what is being done?
Just now, have I suffered!
Just now, have I poured out my innards![27]
'Only through your pains can you relieve our agonies'.

Oh Island,[28] you are soaked in tears!
Scarcely is there one king and everyone wants to be king!
because the sword is used too sparingly.

From now on, this is the Possessor,[29]
whose head, for the disloyal, is surrounded in terror.
The Descendant of the Lion, his head hidden in the shades of night,
defiant once again, shall strive for the stars[30].

The Broken Covenant shall call to anger the Eagle with the Lion Cub[31],
and those who lurk in the forests shall come right up to the (city) walls,
so that the Bulls[32] shall one day fear those whom they hated.

No love between brothers nor true loyalty amongst allies,
No rest, or hardly any, at least, even precarious!

Thorns shall overgrow the willow[33].
Alas! Too much licence will be given to wolves and kites!
'Three times six revolutions, and three more, shall this age last'[34].

---

24 From John's notes and other historical documents, Dr. Padel shows clearly that these ' *six* French-born brothers, the sons of a certain *Toki*, were killed at a place called *Treruf*, somewhere west of St. Michael's Mount, by an uprising of Cornishmen, under the leadership of *Vice-comes Frewin*, in around 1100 AD. This was in revenge for the death of a Cornish land-holder, called Osulf. John says he could say more about this but does not want to make a speech. Frewin is a name found in Cornwall at this period, while *Treruf* is an early form of several Cornish place-names. ;Padel suggests Trereife in Madron. [By coincidence the same name occurs in St. Germans, as Trerieve, but this, of course, is too far east].
25 *solium*, = throne; JC glosses this: *Cornwall*.
    .He adds, 'Also called historically:
    1/. '*Domus Coronei*', the 'House of Coroneus', (companion of Brutus, the refugee from Troy who was said to have given his name to 'Britain'). This story was, I think, entirely invented by Geoffrey, JGH a 2/. the *House of Arcturus*, (Arthur), 'because that most famous of kings came from here'.
26 JC uses the old word for Northern France, Neustria, JGH
27 'For the death of *Osulf*, JC. A land-owner of this name is mentioned in the Domesday Book, JGH
28 Great Britain, JC
29 Probably Stephen, JGH
30 'strive for the greatest things' , JC(i.e. *glory*.
31 i.e. 'The Empress with her brothers', JC
32 '*Bulls*' = *cities*, JC
33 see Note 16
34 (3x6) + 3 = 21 years. If this is for Stephen's reign, it is two years too many, suggesting that Stephen was still king when John wrote. Curley

A Ty Ji Arthur[32], gorrys yn dann vaystri kenedhel fals?,
a ny wel'ta ytho ravnans an gwarthek dre rosow leven Reont[33]?
Pandr'a wre'ta er y bynn?
Hedh, budhek, unn pols!
Praga, a genedhel dhignas,
y hwredh devnydh, yn gis benynreyth, a liw kogh hag a'n jynn-krygh[34]?
Prag y pleg dhis gwiska an bows ornys a gylghyow?
Prag y fynn'ta usya, yn hwyls, euveredhow Gwener?
Kessydhyes osta; unn pla anfeusi usi ow kuhudha pub huni.
Yth esosta a'th worwedh, digolonn,
marnas ty a dheffo ha tenna hebaska
drefenn an Loskvann[35], an Esow, an Klevesow,
ha'n diwettha gwallow a wra dha Rann
dhe vrasa warbarth er dha bynn,
ymons i ow kweskel yn kettella
dha gevrennogyon!

Ottomma unn prys yn distryppyans y das,
yn unn dremena dres kolgh Neb a wyskko an Basnet[36],
an Den Koth Dewisys[37],
lughes a-dro dh'y benn kales,
a wra rosya ryb pennfentynyow an Perydhon.
Pana studh ymava? Pana wovenek yn agan askorr?
Kethwas po marow mara pydh,
pythow po hanow da mara's hepkorr,
sevelyek vydh gwelhevin[38] Vreten.

---

32 'Chi Arthur', 'drefenn bos genys omma an myghtern na a'n moyha bri', JK
33 *Reont* o roswyth war Avon Dee y'n oryon Kembra
34 An Normanyon a dheuth gans gisyow 'benowek', JGH (Poken, esa ev ow skrifa erbynn an vyghternes, Matilda)? - JGH
35 An *loskvann* hag erell = '*an sowson*', JK
36 menydh ughel yn Alban - Alanus de Insula (= DeLisle - ha notenn 59 JGH)
37 Jowann a re omma an geryow yn y vammskrif an pyth a dreylyas yn 'Den Koth Dewisys':
MICHTIERN LUCHD MAL IGASUET'.
Flobert a aswonnis omma hen gernewek rag: 'Myghtern loes avel y gasek'.;
yn prov, skrifys yw an lavar ma gans Jowann, yn Latin, (notenn 58). - JGH
38 JK a skrif '*menydhyow* Alban, kyn styr ev an lavar, yn notenn, *gwelhevin Bow Sows*!.

Oh Thou, House of Arthur, placed in the power of a treacherous[35] people,
canst thou not see, then, the seizure of cattle on the plains of Reont[36]?
What are you doing, to stop it? Pause, Victress, for a moment!
Why, like a woman, do you adorn yourself with rouge and curling-tongs?
Why are you pleased to wear a dress decorated with circles?
Why do you like making yourself up with the vanities of Venus[37]?

You are punished: a single unfortunate Plague attacks us all;
You lie, in despair, unless you can take consolation from the fact
That the same fires, famine, diseases[38],
and the latest evils that thy fate can conjure up against thee,
also strike thy allies[39] in exactly the same way!

    Here for once, in the pillage of his father,
passing over the hood of the Helmeted One[40],
the Chosen Old Man[41], with the lightning playing around his hard head,
shall stroll beside the springs of Periron[42].
What shape is he in? What hope in our offspring?
Come slavery or death, if he loses fame and fortune,
the Nobles of England[43] shall stand aside;

---

35 'It is not useful for me to define this treachery', JC. John says that this concerned a raid by the (Saxon) 'men of Devon' Much more was written here, in the British language, but John omitted it 'so as not to seem abusive'. in the Dedication, John says he is leaving out events following 'Konan's 'lamentable exit', up to William I's time, 'until he knew how his work was received'. The '*exit*' was the massive migration of Britons, led by Conan Meriadoc, which founded Brittany, in the 5th and 6th centuries, but left much of Britannia too weak to repel the Saxons, JGH

36 *Rhyd Reont*, the ford of Reont, is mentioned in several Welsh poems and is thought to be *Vadum Regionis* on the River Dee.

37 The Normans brought 'effeminate' costumes and a fashion for permed hair, JGH

38 JC quotes his source here, giving us the phrase, '*guent dehil*', meaning 'a wind that strips the trees bare of leaves'. T Saunders recognized this as modern Cornish 'gwyns del'. The final *t* in John's phrase proves this to be Old Cornish, (before c. 1200), (unless it is Breton., which kept the 't'), JGH.

39 A gloss here, '*the Saxons*', must surely refer to the plague, rather than the 'allies' JGH .

40 The '*helmeted One*', a mountain in Scotland, Alanus de Insula.

41 JC gives us the phrase in the original: '*michtiern luchd mal igasuet*'. Leon Flobert saw that this was a miscopying of what, in today's Cornish, would be '*Myghtern Loes avel y Gasek*', (i.e. 'A king, as grey as his mare'). Clearly the note was copied out of place, since it does not match John's Latin at this point . Flobert is proved correct for, at MS p. 1, l. 56, John gives us that exact phrase, turned into Latin. Note 63 'grey king', a figure from Celtic mythology, occurs in Welsh prophecies. He may represent 'winter', JGH

42 Periron JC identifies this as the stream that flows past Tintagel. It is obvious, from Welsh texts, that *Periron* (or '*Peryddon*') was an important boundary; Could it have meant the Bristol Channel, (which, in a way, could be said to 'flow past Tintagel'? JGH

43 JC wrote *colles Albani translaterales*', which means '*hills that straddle Albany*'. His notes say, however, that it means the '*nobles of ..England*'.

Yn oryon Arvon, an Pla Brest[39] a wrer;
an Askellek [40]a wra fronna an Bath[41]
ha daskorr termyn hy hendas[42].
An neyth ma, an trysa[43], a vydh diswrys arta, peub a'y du.

An vlydhen usi ow nesa[44], Loundres
a syns pyth eus gesys a'n welenn rywvaneth.

Marth o dhymm yn kynsa, ev dhe ragresek;
marth eus dhymm, nessa,
an peswara po an pympes[45] dhe ragresek!

Skon y sev dhiworth dinas an Vrythonyon[46],
heb dhout rag tevi,
bys may teffo an towlwyw ha bos gyw!
Jynn truesi[47] a sevir rag bedh dhe bub huni.
Ankow a vydh kaws avi, na ny vydh sempel furv an mona!

Hogen, dysk an musur, A Gernow, dysk godhevel!
An fleghes y'gan kowel lesk,
re dhaswrellons galarow an Sowson!
Praga mar hel agan leuv?
Piw, a-wosa, a vydh synsys dhe vos rydh?
A-dal an Charet[48], may tiberth alena
an Tamar, war tu'n deghow,
ryb kribennow menydhyow Goen Brenn[49],
gwer Bow Gall a berth an roweth a bub tu!

Mar mynn'ta pesya yn fyw, a Vyghternes,
gonis has a wredh, gans aras;
a'n pris na, pals vydh pub eghenn
a legesser hag a vogh.
Awel Garow[50] ha sordyans a bub sort
a wra annia an bobel,
erna hettho sorr trist an Tarenner.
Kevrennek re bo an genedhel vyghan morethek
a'y vodh da, dyantell,

---

39 = bresel, yn Kembra,- JK
40 Matilda, -JK
41 ? An 'Bath' = Kernow - JGH
42 Henri (I) 'Termyn a gres'- JK
43 An '3a neyth' yw , wosa demmedhi diwweyth, pan hwilas Matilda synsi tron Pow Sows - JK, JGH
44 1141 , pan veu Stephen prisonys yn Lincoln, -JK, JGH.
45 Dout mar pe Gwilym (a'n Gorhel Gwynn) niverys ynter an myghternedh - JK
46 Lundonia - JK; Esa Jowann ow ri dynnargh dhe Stephen, devedhys a Loundres rag daskavoes Kernow? JGH
47 =Tour Loundres - JK
48 Yn sowsnek, 'The great Bear', JGH
49 'y'gan yeth ni, po, yn sowsnek, *Fawi-mor*' - JK. Ny gevir yn nahen tyller an hanow kernewek ma,
50 Jowann a re omma an kernewek: '*Auel garu*'

9

On the shores of Arfon[44], the Brazen Pest[45] is being formed.
The Winged One shall bridle the Boar and bring back the time of her ancestor[46].
This nest, the third[47], shall completely fall apart!
The coming year[48], London shall wield what is left of the Sceptre.
I was amazed firstly, that he took precedence;
I am amazed, secondly, that the fourth or the fifth took precedence[49].
Soon he shall arise from the fortress of the Britons[50],
obviously to grow in stature,
until the javelin becomes a lance!
A melancholy machine[51] shall be raised up, that will be a tomb for everyone.
Death will be a cause of envy[52]. nor will the form of money be simple.

But learn the beat of the dance, Cornwall, learn to suffer![53]
The babes in our cradles shall renew the lamentations of the Saxons!
Why are we so generous?
Who, from now on, shall be considered free?
Opposite the Great Bear, where the Tamar rises,
to flow south, past the tors of Bodmin Moor[54],
the Frenchmen hold power on every hand.
If you wish to stay alive, O Queen, you will plough and sow;
at which cost, all kinds of mouse-traps and buck-goats will multiply.
A wild wind[55] and upheavals of all kinds
shall trouble the people until the miserable rage of the Thunder subsides.
May the unhappy little nation partake of his uncertain favour
and, meanwhile, pray for insignificant blessings on its own account.
Religion weeps: in vain, prays he who wears a habit.

---

44 Arfon, North Wales. For John, this region included Lincoln, where Stephen was taken captive (note 48)!
45 The '*Brazen Pest*' = 'war', JC
46 i.e. 'The Eagle, (The Empress), shall control the king and bring back the peaceful time of her ancestor, Henricus', (Henry I), JC
47 The '*third nest*' was her attempt on the English crown. (the 'second', her second marriage, to Geofffrey of Anjou), JC.
48 'When England was without a king for a year', JC. 1141, when Stephen was captive for nine months, in Lincoln, JGH
49 '*the fourth or the fifth*' , because he is uncertain whether to include William, (drowned in the White Ship, amongst the kings. Geoffrey has a similar riddling phrase, '*From the first to the fourth, from the fourth to the third, from the third to the second, shall the thumb be rolled in oil*' (i.e. 'anointed'). This is usually thought to mean: William I, W II, Henry I and Stephen', JGH
50 This *fortress*: ' i.e. London', JC
51 The '*machine* i.e.' The Tower of London, JC
52 i.e. inmates will wish they were dead, JC
53 'on account of the invaders' greed', JC
54 JC gives the Old Cornish name for Bodmin Moor - known, 'in Saxon' as Fawi Mor, (well-attested), and 'in Britannico', *Goen Bren*. This is clearly recognizable Cornish meaning the 'rough grazing on the hill'. John is the unique source for this information, JGH. Likewise, John's Latin name for the moor, '*Brentigia*' is unknown elsewhere.
55 JC gives 'wild wind' in the Old Cornish - *auel garu*. In 1136, Exeter was captured by Stephen after a three-month siege, during which Baldwin de Redvers held it for Matilda. This section seems to refer to the attacks on the Church, in 1140. Reginald, Matilda's half-brother, Earl of Cornwall, was excommunicated. Also to the conflict between him and Stephen's preference, Alan of Dinan, Count of Brittany and Earl of Richmond. JGH

hag, yn unn wortos,
pysadow distyr re wrello
a -berth dhedhi hy honan.

Kryjyans a oel; yn euver, y pys neb a wyskko gon.
Neb a wra dhe'n Nev treylya, y klyw.
Neb a dewl taran, y klyw.

War tu ha'n howlsedhes,
Iwerdhon a goedh dhe'n Hweghes[51].
Yn askra Gorlewin, yth hedh askorr an Gogledh[52].

Ha prag, mar dhiwedhes, tyli dhe'n Dinas Anfeusik[53]?
Pan esa kummyas dhe'n skoes,
y'n eur-na, yth o dhe les
delivra pris an trumach.
Yw ev dhe voy gwiw y wormel
rag y lender dhe Dhyw
pyneyl rag y obereth yn arvow?
Ow tiswul fosow, ow treylya kelliow dhe woenyow?,
Noeth-he a wra an menydhyow
ha nowydh-he rewlow ha'n lagha.

Neb a worro a-dro dh'y dhiwglun
eskelli , a veu parys, treghys dhe ves,
hag, yn y wols, kribenn lew,
surra a gerensa an bobel,
y trehedh, yn unn nija, an tiredh ughel;
pur wir, diberth a wra templys an dus sans;
na ny dhannvon an Dhragon
myghternedh lagasek y'n gwel.
Y tesedh pows dhe'n sitys,
gans gemmow dynyus
ha, heudhik, y hwra ranna rohow
yntra gwyrghes.
Wosa henna, ow hwiles onan anedha,
y's demmedh yn lowen.

"Saw nebes y fydh blydhynyow hemma
hag uskis dhe'n re vyghan!"

---

51 Ny yll an 'hweghes' bos Henri II, marnas nebonan dhe geworra an linenn, yn unn wul dasskrif. - JGH
52 An Normanyon
53 JK a re hanow an 'Dinas': *Aschbiri*, po 'in Britannico', *Cair Belli*, po *Castel Uchel Coed*. Martesen, Car Billy, Blisland, po Carbeile, Penntor? Castel Uchel Coed yw fest haval dhe *Caruggatt*, (Ker ughel goes) ogas dhe Jiwardreth (hag *Uhelgoad* yn Breten Vyghan) - JGH

Thou that makest the heavens to turn, hearest us!
Thou that wieldest the thunderbolts, hearest us!

To the Westward, Ireland shall fall to the Sixth[56].
To the West, reach out the progeny of the North[57].
Why, so late, pay the ominous castle[58]?
When there was licence to the shield, then it was some use paying the fare.

Should he be more praised for his faithfulness to God
or for his feats of arms?
Dismantling walls and turning woodland into heath,
he will lay bare the hills and renew the laws and regulations.

He who puts on his flanks, wings that were cut off, ready,
and, in his hair, a lion's mane,
more sure of the people's affection,
shall fly right up to the highlands,
and, truly, shall separate the temples from the holy men;
nor shall the Dragon send out a wise king into the pastures.
He will deck out cities with alluring gems,
and, happily, distribute gifts amongst the virgins.
After that, selecting one of them, he will gladly marry her.

But brief will be his years and fleeting, for the little ones!
Go, Days of the Lynx!
The German dragon will be ashamed
that Thou and thy Gods crossed our frontiers[59].
It will fly into a rage and act for itself.

Why has Normandy arisen more slowly?
Like an old buttress, Britain will put on its old name[60].
Let it go its own way. May my race put an end to hers![61]

---

56 If this means Henry II, it must be a later insertion. JGH
57 'The Normans', JC
58 This 'castle' is named by JC as '*Aschbiri*, or, 'in British', *Cair Belli* , 'or, as some people prefer', '*Castel Uchel Coed*, (the 'castle in the high wood'. This information is very ambiguous; the Breton scholar, Joseph Loth, thought it referred to a large hill-fort near Week St. Mary, but I can find no evidence for this. *Cair Belli*, i.e. the fort of a chieftain called Beli, could refer to Car Billy, near Blisland, or else Carbeile, near Torpoint. As for the 'castle in the high wood', Geoffrey, following Nennius, took a name quite like this, to mean Exeter! But the old Celtic name for that city is well-known; Asser, in his 9th C. Life of Alfred, records it as 'Cair Uuisc', and the name was still used in 17th C Cornish, spelt *Karesk*. One or two places in Cornwall fit much better, notably '*Caruggatt*, near Tywardreath, which means exactly, 'The fort in the high wood'. Also compare the name of the town, *Uhelgoad*, in Brittany, JGH
59 JC notes here, about the Saxons, '*For they were idolatrous when they arrived, and for many years afterwards*'
60 Its 'old name' is *Britain*. This is made explicit in Geofrey's treatment of a similar passage: 'Nomine Bruti vocabitur et nuncupatio extraneorum peribit' Bk 7, l. 110 - Curley
61 '*hers*' must mean the *Saxon race*.

Kewgh, dydhyow an Lynks! Pryvenn[54] re berthi meth
drefenn ha Ty ha'th Tywow[55] dhe dremena agan oryon.
Honna a gemmer sorr hag a ober rygdhi hy honan.

Prag yth omsevis Neustria dhe voy lent?
Avel hen goloven, re dhrollo Breten[56] yn mes hy hen hanow.
Res ello yn hy fordh hy honan;
ow agh re lattho hy huni.

Sewen re bo an gewer;
Konan[57] a wra goelya an tonnow;
Neb a re gorhemmynadow dhe'n Barth Kledh,
re weresso dhe Gadwalader;
An Myghtern, Loes avel y Gasek Erghwynn[58],
oll warbarth herwydh y dhevar,
wosa treylya hyns Fros Perydhon[59],
ow kannhe gans y welenn rywvaneth,
y syns an livow yn kres kylgh
hag a vusur melin dresta.

---

54 = an Sowson - JK
55 An sowson o termyn hir heb kristoneth.- JK
56 Jeffri, y'n tyller ma, a brev bos hemma styr an linenn: ev a lever '*nomen Brut'i*. JGH
57 Konan (Conan Meriadoc) a Vreten Vyghan) ha Kadwalader (an ' evellyon'), pupprys an selwadoryon vrythonek. JGH
58 (ha notenn 37): y kevir an person ma , (?' = *Gwav* - JGH) 'y'n bardhonek kembrek, '*Brut Dingestow*'.
59 *Peryddon*, po *Periron*: tyller a vri, (yn oryon Kembra?). Kyn lever JK y vos hanow dowr byghan heb hanow, usi ow resek ryb *Dindaiol* (Tintagel). A yll e bos an hen hanow a rann an Havren (The Bristol Channel)?) - JGH

May the weather be fine; Konan[62] shall sail the waves.
May Kadwalader receive help from him who gives orders to the North.

The king, as white-haired as his snow-white mare[63],
having, all in the ‚line of duty, altered the course of the stream of Periron,

shall gather the floods in the middle of a circle,
and, with his whitening sceptre,
measure out a mill across them.

After so many disasters and so much repeated suffering,
the Severn will hear as amany trumpets;
after so many battles mixed in them,
thy waters, Oh Tavy[64], shall laugh!

Again, the thorns shall tremble; the Twins[65] shall set up their tents.
First here, then there, the first things are due to be paid to Reont![66]
Javelins , pikes, swords and darts shall the enemy receive in their warm flanks.
Blood will flow in waves and discolour the rivers!
Joyful the waves, and joyful, as I can vouch for it, the sands!

Happy were the Saxon tyrants, if only they had let go earlier!
Those who are worthy of their steeds[67] and eager with their lances,
draw near, man to man;
only a few, forgetting how to win, will abandon their colours.
For shame! Out of the eighteen thousand who were there just a moment before, four will turn their backs, to run away in disgrace![68]'

---

62 'Konan' is the legendary founder of Brittany who here joins with Kadwalader, the great Welsh hero, in a united front to liberate Britain from the English, JGH
63 See Note 41
64 'Tavy'. This may be what JC had in mind when he wrote *Thevi*, but, if the original for this part of the Prophecy was Welsh, the source may have meant the River Teifi, (in Wales, like, probably, .*Reont*).
65 'The Twins', i.e. Konan and Kadwalader, JGH
66 Latin: debentur prima Reonti: Here I follow Leon Flobert. Tim Saunders suggests: 'The first things are paid to Reont'.
67 'worthy of their steeds': There is an old Breton personal name, *Guilligomarc'h*, which may mean exactly that; also, compare *Wiomarc'h*, king of Brittany in 822 AD - JGH.
68 These exact figures come from the '*Armes Prydain*', a 10th century Welsh prophecy on the same subject, i.e. the '*spes britannorum*', the hoped-for ecovery of the island by its original inhabitants. That poem also features Konan and Kadwalader as leaders.

Wosa mar lies terros
ha poenow, menowgh godhevys,
an Havren a glywvydh keniver korn;
rag bos kemmyskys ynna i mar lies kevammok ,
A Tavi[60], dha dhowrow a hwerth!

Hwath, an dreyn a gren; an Evellyon a sett aga thyldys.
Treweythyow ena, treveth arall enos,
i a dal an kynsa taklow dhe Reont[61]!
Y tegemmer an eskerens, y'ga thenewenn toemm,
towlwywow, pikow, kledhedhyow ha sethigow!
Krow a wra devera yn tonnow
ha disliwa an avonyow.
Lowenek an tonnow,
lowenek, ha my yn test, an tewosow!

Da via gans an durans sowsnek
a kwrellens hepkorr kyns!
An re na, gwiw a'ga margh[62],
freth aga gywow, y nesons, korf orth korf;
ny wra saw nebes ankevi fatell fetha
ha gasa aga banerow;
rag meth! yn mysk etek mil[63],
esa ena nammnygen,
peswar a dreyl keyn,
dignas, rag omdenna!

---

60 'Thevi' JK; poken, martesen, an avon *Teifi*, yn Kembra, JGH
61 neb unn roswyth, yn oryon Kembra
62 nb: an hanow koth ,Bretonek,: *Guilligomar* (Gwiw aga margh); nb *Wiomarc'h*, myghtern a Vreten Vyghan yn 822 wosa Krist - JGH
63 An niverow ma a veu kemmerys dhiworth an profoesa kembrek, '*Armes Prydein*', (930 wosa Krist)- JGH

This is what Gwynedd wanted, truly.
It is raised up again, right up to its gilded tip,
and shall lead the peoples to unity.
Women will exchange fleeces for purple cloth;
men shall put on the silver that has been extracted by Caerleon
The valleys shall rise up and the oaks too shall be verdant[69]!
The mountains of Arfon shall reach the clouds with their peaks.
Posterity shall raise up the Royal Diadem of the GreatBriton.
The good looks of the leaders shall spread to deserved honours.
The marvellous handsomeness of the Two
shall extend to common tasks.

'Three hundred and sixty three years[70] shall see the end
of a Golden Age, the colour of Heaven'.

Here endeth
The prophecy of Ambrosius Merlinus, concerning the Seven Kings[71].

---

69 Geoffrey specifies 'The *Cornish Oaks*'; it is strange that John did not pick this up. Is it possible that Geoffrey, an inventive romancer, added this detail himself?
70 The combination of 'three' s is typical of Celtic prophetic verse.
71 'The seven kings': John has taken, and in some cases, amended, the prophecy so that it applies to the first Norman rulers, but ends, of course, with Konan and Kadwalader, the'Two'. It is possible that these 'seven kings' originally referred to a local Welsh dynasty.

Otta'n pyth a vynna Gwynedh
ha, dhe wir, dassevys bys y'n penn gorowrys,
hi a led an poblow bys unnses.

Benyn a wra kestreylya knyv
erbynn dhillas pannow purpur!
Den a wra gwiska an arghans
a wrug Kerleghyon[64] dhe strotha.

An nansow a sev ha'n derwennow ynwedh a wra glasa;[65]
barrow Arvon[66] a dhrehedh an kommol ;

y trehev henedhow a syw
kurun ryw an Brython Meur[67]!
Tekter marthys an hembrenkysi a yskynn
dhe enorow dendilys.
Kaderder marthys an Dhew a wra gorfenna
yn obereth kemmyn.

"Tri hans, tri ugens ha teyr blydhen[68]
y tiwedh rydhses owrek
rag oes kevliw ha'n Nev."

Yma omma ow tiwedha

Dargan Verdhin[69] yn kever an Seyth Myghtern.

---

64 ?Chester - JGH
65 Jeffri Monow a skrif: 'derwennow *Kernow*'. Koynt yw Jowann dhe asa henna yn mes - JGH
66 Kembra gledh
67 Rag '*Breten Veur*' ? - JGH
68 nb Lies '*tri*', gorrys warbarth, herwydh gnas hen geltek - JGH
69 *Merlinus Ambrosius*, skrifys yn Latin

Rol berr erthyglow ha lyvrow dhe les

Some useful background reading

A New Edition of John of Cornwall's Prophecy of Merlin
    (Latin text and notes), Editor Michael Curley Speculum, 572, 1982

Armes Prydain ed. Sir Ifor Williams,   Dublin, 1972

Historia Regum Britanniae, Geoffrey of Monmouth,   Penguin Classics, 1966

Geoffrey of Monmouth - and Cornwall O.J. Padel
                               Cambridge Medieval Celtic Studies no 8, 1984

Vita Merlini, Geoffrey of Monmouth,   Ed. JJ Parry, University of Illinois, 1925

French translation and notes   Fleuriot & Flobert, Etudes Celtiques, 1974

The Legendary History of Britain,   JSP Tatlock

Early Vaticination in Welsh, Enid Griffiths,   Cardiff, 1937

The Quest for Merlin,   Nikolai Tolstoy, Sceptre 1989

Celt and Saxon,   Peter Berresford Ellis, Constable & Co Ltd., 1993

Rag derivadow war an yeth kernewek ha rol gwerthow
For information on the Cornish language and a sales list
dannvon dhe
send to:

Kesva an Taves Kernewek
The Cornish Language Board
65 Churchtown
Gwynnyer/*Gwinear*
Heyl/*Hayle*
Kernow TR27 5JL

☎ 01736 850878

Kowethas an Yeth Kernewek
The Cornish Language Fellowship
Fentenwynn
Bre Wartha/*Top Hill*
Fordh Ponsmeur/*Grampound Road*
Truro/*Truro*
Kernow TR2 4DR

☎ 01726 882681

An Dhargan a Verdhin
The Prophecy of Merlin

Jowann Kernow
John of Cornwall

Dyllans kernewek ha sowsnek gans

Edition in Cornish and English by

Julyan Holmes

~wek,
1998

Hedra
er 2001

Kudhlenn (cover pictu~),. ~nsyn Moore

ISBN 1 902917 197